a little brown notebook

Scenes from
The Secret Garden
by Frances Hodgson Burnett

Illustrated by Gordon Parker

A Sterling/Museum Quilts Book
Sterling Publishing Co., Inc. New York

There was something mysterious in the air that morning. Nothing was done in its regular order and several of the nativ servants seemed missing, while those whom Mary saw slunk or hurried about with ashy and scared faces. But no one would tell her anything, and her Ayah did not come.

'Is it so very bad?'

'Awfully, Mrs. Lennox. You ought to have gone to the hills two weeks ago.'

'Oh, I know I ought!' she cried. 'I only stayed to go to that silly dinner-party.'

...The cholera had broken out in its most fatal form and people were dying like flies...

During the confusion and bewilderment of the second day Mary hid herself in the nursery and was forgotten by everyone. Nobody thought of her, nobody wanted her, and strange things happened of which she knew nothing.

'...There is a child here! A child alone! In a place like this! Mercy on us, who is she?'

'I am Mary Lennox, I fell asleep when everyone had the cholera and I have only just wakened up. Why does nobody come?'

It was in that strange and sudden way that Mary found out that she had neither father nor mother left; that they had died and been carried away in the night, and that the few native servants who had not died also had left the house as quickly as they could get out of it...

She knew that she was not going to stay at the English clergyman's house where she was taken at first...
The English clergyman was poor and he had five children nearly all the same age and they wore shabby clothes and were always quarrelling...

'You are going to be sent home,' Basil said to her, 'at the end of the week. And we're glad of it.'

'I am glad of it, too,' answered Mary. 'Where is home?'

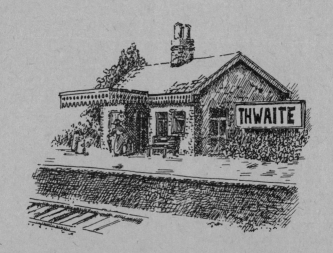

'She doesn't know where home is!' said Basil, with seven-year-old scorn. 'It's England of course...You are going to your uncle. His name is Mr. Archibald Craven...He lives in a great, big, desolate old house in the country, and no one goes near him...he's a hunch-back...'

Mary made the long voyage to England under the care of an officer's wife...Mr. Archibald Craven sent to meet her in London.

The woman was his housekeeper at Misselthwaite Manor, and her name was Mrs. Medlock.

'Captain Lennox and his wife died of the cholera,' Mr. Craven had said in his short, cold way. 'Captain Lennox was my wife's brother and I am their daughter's guardian. The child is to be brought here. You must go to London and bring her yourself.'

...Mary felt as if the drive would never come to an end, and that the wide, bleak moor was a wide expanse of black ocean through which she was passing on a strip of dry land.

The entrance door was a huge one made of massive, curiously shaped panels of oak studded with big iron nails and bound with great iron bars. It opened into an enormous hall, which was so dimly lighted that the faces in the portraits on the walls and the figures in the suits of armour made Mary feel that she did not want to look at them.

'Are you going to be my servant?' Mary asked, still in her imperious little Indian way.

Martha began to rub her grate again.

'I'm Mrs. Medlock's servant?' she said stoutly. 'An' she's Mr. raven's—but I'm to do the housemaid's work up here an' wait on you a bit. But you won't need much waiting on.'

'Who is going to dress me?' demanded Mary.

'Canna' tha' dress thysen!'

'No,' answered Mary, quite indignantly. 'I never did it in my life. My Ayah dressed me, of course.'

'You thought I was a native! You dared! You don't know anything about natives! They are not people—they're servants who must salaam to you.'

It had not been the custom that Mistress Mary should do anything but stand and allow herself to be dressed like a doll, but before she was ready for breakfast she began to suspect that her life at Misselthwaite Manor would end by teaching her a number of things quite new to her...

...If Martha had been a well-trained fine young lady's-maid she would have been more subservient and respectful and would have known that it was her business to brush hair, and button boots, and pick things up and lay them away.

...She was, however, only an untrained Yorkshire rustic who had been brought up in a moorland cottage with a swarm of little brothers and sisters who had never dreamed of doing anything but waiting on themselves and on the younger ones who were either babies in arms or just learning to totter about and tumble over things.

'...There's twelve of us an' my father only gets sixteen shilling a week. I can tell you my mother's put to it to get porridge for 'em all. They tumble about on th' moor an' play there all day, an' mother says th' air of th' moor fattens 'em.'

'One of th' gardens is locked up. No one has been in it for ten years.'

'Mr. Craven had it shut when his wife died so sudden. He won't let no one go inside. It was her garden. He locked th' door an' dug a hole and buried th' key.'

'What is your name?' Mary inquired.

He stood up to answer her.

'Ben Weatherstaff,' he answered, and then he added with a surly chuckle, 'I'm lonely mysel' except when he's with me,' and he jerked his thumb toward the robin. 'He's th' only friend I've got.'

'Tha' an' me are a good bit alike,' he said. 'We was wove out of th' same cloth. We're neither of us good-looking an' we're both of us as sour as we look. We've got the same nasty tempers, both of us, I'll warrant.'

'Would you make friends with me?' she said to the robin,
just as if she were speaking to a person. 'Would you?'

Mary did not shout, but she looked at things. There was nothing else to do. She walked round and round the gardens and wandered about the paths in the park.

'It's very queer,' she said. 'Ben Weatherstaff said there was no door and there is no door. But there must have been one ten years ago, because Mr. Craven buried the key.'

At that moment a very good thing was happening to her. Four good things had happened to her, in fact, since she came to Misselthwaite Manor. She had felt as if she had understood a robin and that he had understood her; she had run in the wind until her blood had grown warm; she had been healthily hungry for the first time in her life; and she had found out what it was to be sorry for some one. She was getting on.

'Do you hear anyone crying?' she said.
Martha suddenly looked confused.
'No,' she answered. 'It's th' wind.'

'But listen,' said Mary. 'It's in the house—down one of
those long corridors.'

Something troubled and awkward in her manner made
Mistress Mary stare very hard at her. She did not believe she
was speaking the truth.

...she opened more doors and more. She saw so many room
that she became quite tired and began to think that there
must be a hundred, though she had not counted them. In a
of them there were old pictures or old tapestries with strang
scenes worked on them.

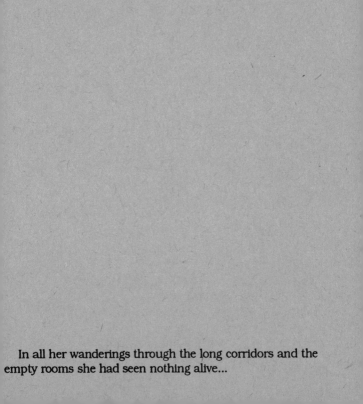

In all her wanderings through the long corridors and the empty rooms she had seen nothing alive...

'What are you doing here?'...'I didn't know which way to go and I heard someone crying.'

She quite hated Mrs. Medlock at the moment, but she hated her more the next.

'You didn't hear anything of the sort,' said the housekeeper. 'You come along back to your own nursery or I'll box your ears.'

Mary looked at it, not really knowing why the hole was there, and as she looked she saw something almost buried in the newly turned soil. It was something like a ring of rusty iron or brass, and when the robin flew up into a tree near by she put out her hand and picked the ring up.

...It was more than a ring, however; it was an old key which looked as if it had been buried a long time...

'Perhaps it is the key to the garden!'

She took the key in her pocket when she went back to the
~~ouse~~, and she made up her mind that she would always
~~arry~~ it with her when she went out, so that if she ever should
~~nd~~ the hidden door she would be ready.

'...I've brought thee a present.'

It was a strong, slender rope with a striped red and blue handle at each end, but Mary Lennox had never seen a skipping-rope before. She gazed at it with a mystified expression.

The skipping-rope was a wonderful thing. She counted and skipped, and skipped and counted, until her cheeks were quite red, and she was more interested than she had ever been since she was born.

.Upon my word! P'raps tha' art a young 'un, after all, an' raps tha's got child's blood in thy veins instead of sour uttermilk. Tha's skipped red into thy cheeks as sure as my ame's Ben Weatherstaff. I wouldn't have believed tha' could o it.'

when she saw the robin she laughed again.

'You showed me where the key was yesterday,' she said. 'You ought to show me the door to-day; but I don't believe you know!'

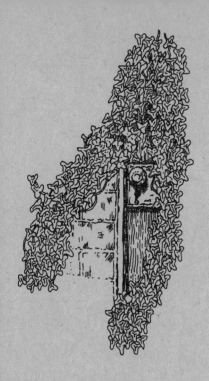

...a round knob which had been covered by the leaves hanging over it. It was the knob of a door.

It was the lock of the door which had been closed ten years, and she put her hand in her pocket, drew out the key, and found it fitted the keyhole. She put the key in and turned it. It took two hands to do it, but it did turn.

She was standing *inside* the secret garden.

was the sweetest, most mysterious-looking place anyone
ould imagine. The high walls which shut it in were covered
th the leafless stems of climbing roses, which were so thick
at they matted together.

'How still it is!' she whispered. 'How still!' ...'No wonder it is still,' she whispered again. 'I am the first person who has spoken in here for ten years.'

...Everything was strange and silent, and she seemed to be hundreds of miles away from anyone, but somehow she did not feel lonely at all. All that troubled her was her wish that she knew whether all the roses were dead, or if perhaps some of them had lived and might put out leaves and buds as the weather got warmer. She did not want it to be a quite dead garden.

She went from place to place, and dug and weeded, and enjoyed herself so immensely that she was led on from bed to bed and into the grass under the trees.

The robin was tremendously busy. He was very much pleased to see gardening begun on his own estate.

My dear Dickon:
    This comes hoping to find you well as it leaves me at present. Miss Mary has plenty of money and will you go to Thwaite and buy her some flower seeds and a set of garden tools to make a flower-bed. Pick the prettiest ones and easy to grow because she has never done it before and lived in India which is different...

            Your loving sister,

                    Martha Phoebe Sowerby

.A boy was sitting under a tree, with his back against it, playing on a rough wooden pipe. He was a funny-looking boy about twelve. He looked very clean and his nose turned up and his cheeks were as red as poppies, and never had Mistress Mary seen such round and such blue eyes in any boy's face.

'I'm Dickon,' the boy said, 'I know tha'rt Miss Mary.'

'I've got th' garden tools. There's a little spade an' rake an' a fork an' hoe...There's a trowel, too. An' th' woman in th' shop threw in a packet o' white poppy an' one o' blue larkspur when I bought th' other seeds.'

'Could you keep a secret, if I told you one? It's a great secret. I don't know what I should do if anyone found it out. I believe I should die!'

'I'm keepin' secrets all th' time,' he said. 'If I couldn't keep secrets from th' other lads, secrets about foxes' cubs, an' birds' nests, an' wild things' holes, there'd be naught safe on th' moor. Aye, I can keep secrets.'

'I've stolen a garden,' she said very fast. 'It isn't mine. It isn't anybody's. Nobody wants it, nobody cares for it, nobody ever goes into it. Perhaps everything is dead in it already; I don't know.'

'...It's a secret garden, and I'm the only one in the world who wants it to be alive.'

'Eh!' he almost whispered, 'it is a queer, pretty place. It's like as if a body was in a dream.'

'Eh! The nests as'll be here come springtime,' he said. 'It'd be th' safest nestin' place in England. No one never comin' near an' tangles o' trees an' roses to build in. I wonder all th' birds on th' moor don't build here.'

'There's a lot of work to do here!' he said once, looking about quite exultantly. 'Will you come again and help me do it?' Mary begged...

'I'll come every day if tha' wants me, rain or shine,' he answered stoutly. 'It's th' best fun I ever had in my life shut, in here an' wakenin' up a garden.'

'It's a secret garden sure enough,' he said, 'but seems like someone besides th' robin must have been in it since it was shut up ten year' ago...as if there'd been a bit o' prunin' done here an' there, later than ten year' ago.'

'Dickon,' she said. 'You are as nice as Martha said you ere. I like you, and you make the fifth person. I never ought I should like five people.'

'Your mother and Martha,' Mary checked them off on her fingers, 'and the robin and Ben Weatherstaff.'

'...Mr. Craven came back this mornin' and I think he wants to see you.'

Mary turned quite pale.

...She could see that the man in the chair was not so much a hunchback as a man with high, rather crooked shoulders, and he had black hair streaked with white.

'Don't look so frightened,' he exclaimed. '...I am your guardian, though I am a poor one for any child. I cannot give you time or attention. I am too ill, and wretched and distracted; but I wish you to be happy and comfortable...Is there anything you want?'

'Might I,' quavered Mary, 'might I have a bit of earth? ...To plant seeds in—to make things grow—to see them come alive, Mary faltered.

'You can have as much earth as you want,' he said. 'You remind me of someone else who loved the earth and things that grow. When you see a bit of earth you want,' with something like a smile, 'take it, child, and make it come alive.'

She had been lying awake, turning from side to side for about an hour, when suddenly something made her sit up in bed and turn her head toward the door listening.

'That isn't the wind. It is different. It is that crying I heard before.'

'I am going to find out what it is,' she said. 'Everybody is in bed and I don't care about Mrs. Medlock—I don't care!'

.The far-off faint crying went on and led her.

...There was a low fire glowing faintly on the hearth and a night-light burning by the side of a carved four-posted bed hung with brocade, and on the bed was lying a boy, crying pitifully.

'Who are you?' he said at last in a half-frightened whisper. 'Are you a ghost?'

'No, I am not,' Mary answered, her own whisper sounding half-frightened. 'Are you one?'

'I am Colin Craven. Who are you?'
'I am Mary Lennox. Mr. Craven is my uncle.'
'He is my father,' said the boy.
...'No one ever told me he had a boy! Why didn't they?'

'Because I am like this always, ill and having to lie down...If I live I may be a hunchback, but I shan't live. My father hates to think I may be like him.'

'Oh, what a queer house this is!' Mary said. 'What a queer house? Everything is a kind of secret. Rooms are locked up and gardens are locked up—and you! Have you been locked up?'

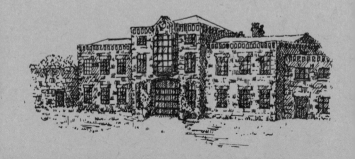

'Does your father come and see you?' Mary ventured.

'Sometimes. Generally when I am asleep. He doesn't want to see me...My mother died when I was born and it makes him wretched to look at me. He thinks I don't know, but I've heard people talking. He almost hates me.'

'...If you are real, sit down on that big footstool and talk. I want to hear about you.'

Though his father rarely saw him when he was awake, he was given all sorts of wonderful things to amuse himself with. He never seemed to have been amused, however.

'I am ten...and so are you.'

'How do you know that?' he demanded in a surprised voice.

'Because when you were born the garden door was locked and the key was buried. And it has been locked for ten years.'

'...My doctor is my father's cousin. He is quite poor and if I die he will have all Misselthwaite when my father is dead. I should think he wouldn't want me to live.'

'They have to please me,' he said. 'I will make them take me there and I will let you go, too.'

'Oh, don't—don't—don't do that!' she cried...'if you make them open the door and take you in like that it will never be a secret again.'

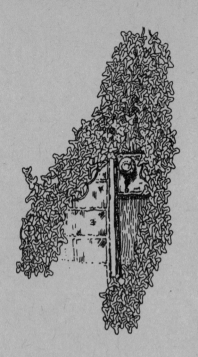

'If you won't make them take you to the garden,' pleaded Mary, 'perhaps—I feel almost sure I can find out how to get in sometime. And then—if the doctor wants you to go out in your chair, and if you can always do what you want to do, perhaps we might find some boy who would push you and w would go alone and it always be a secret garden.'

'I am going to let you look at something,' he said. 'Do you see that rose-coloured silk curtain hanging on the wall over the mantelpiece? There is a cord hanging from it...Go and pull it.'

'...Why is the curtain drawn over her?'
'...Sometimes I don't like to see her looking at me. She smiles too much when I am ill and miserable. Besides, she is mine and I don't want everyone to see her.'

'I wish I could go to sleep before you leave me,' he said rather shyly.

'Shut your eyes,' said Mary, drawing her footstool closer, 'and I will do what my Ayah used to do in India. I will pat your hand and stroke it and sing something quite low.'

'I have found out what the crying was...It was Colin. I
ound him.'

'Miss Mary! ...Tha' shouldn't have done it—tha' shouldn't! Tha'll get me in trouble. I never told thee nothin' about him—but tha'll get me in trouble. I shall lose my place and what'll Mother do!'

'...If Mrs. Medlock finds out, she'll think I broke orders and told thee and I shall be packed back to Mother.'

'He is not going to tell Mrs. Medlock anything about it yet. It's to be a sort of secret just at first,' said Mary firmly. 'And he says everybody is obliged to do as he pleases.'

'Aye, that's true enough—th' bad lad!' sighed Martha...

'What is the matter with him?' asked Mary.

'Mr. Craven went off his head like when he was born...Th' doctors thought he'd have to be put in a 'sylum. It was because Mrs. Craven died like I told you. He wouldn't set eyes on th' baby. He just raved and said it'd be another hunchback like him and it'd better die.'

'Who is Dickon? What a queer name!'

'He is Martha's brother. He is twelve years old,' she explained. 'He is not like anyone else in the world. He can charm foxes and squirrels and birds just as the natives in India charm snakes.'

They enjoyed themselves so much that they forgot the pictures and they forgot about the time. They had been laughing quite loudly over Ben Weatherstaff and his robin, and Colin was actually sitting up as if he had forgotten about his weak back when he suddenly remembered something.

'Do you know there is one thing we have never once thought of?' he said. 'We are cousins.'

.And in the midst of the fun the door opened, and in walked
r. Craven and Mrs. Medlock.

Dr. Craven started in actual alarm and Mrs. Medlock almost fell back because he had accidentally bumped against her.

...She had spent hours of every day with Colin in his room, talking about rajahs or gardens or Dickon and the cottage on the moor. They had looked at the splendid books and pictures and sometimes Mary had read things to Colin, and sometimes he had read a little to her.

.There is something I want to tell you...do you know about
olin? He says I'm making him forget about being ill and
ving.'

'...I was wonderin' if us could ever get him in th' humour to come out here an' lie under th' trees in his carriage...I've wondered if we could bring him here without anyone seeing us. I thought perhaps you could push his carriage.'

'Mr. Craven sent it to you,' said Martha...She opened the package...There were several beautiful books such as Colin had...There were two or three games...and there was a beautiful little writing case with a gold monogram on it and a gold pen and ink-stand.

..she was awakened by such dreadful sounds that she jumped out of the bed in an instant.

'It's Colin...He's having one of those tantrums the nurse calls hysterics...He'll do himself harm. No one can do anything with him. You come and try, like a good child. He likes you.'

.You stop!' she almost shouted. 'You stop! I hate you! everybody hates you! I wish everybody would run out of the ouse and let you scream yourself to death! You *will* scream ourself to death in a minute, and I wish you would!'

'If you scream another scream,' she said, 'I'll scream, too—
and I can scream louder than you can, and I'll frighten you,
I'll frighten you!'

'...Half that ails you is hysterics and temper—just hysterics—hysterics—hysterics!' and she stamped each time she said it.

'I felt the lump! I shall have a hunch on my back and then I shall die,' and he began to writhe again and turned on his face and sobbed and wailed, but he didn't scream.

'You didn't feel a lump!' contradicted Mary fiercely... 'Hysterics makes lumps. There's nothing the matter with your horrid back—nothing but hysterics!'

...He put out his hand a little toward Mary, and I am glad to say that, her own tantrum having passed, she was softened too, and met him half-way with her hand, so that it was a sort of making up.

'...I brought these two in my pockets. This one here he's called
Nut an' this here other one's called Shell.'

..Eh! my! we mun get him out here—we mun get him watchin' an' listenin' an' sniffin' up th' air an' get him just soaked through wi' sunshine. An' we munnot lose no time about it.'

Dickon came in smiling his nicest wide smile. The new-born lamb was in his arms and the little red fox trotted by his side. Nut sat on his left shoulder and Soot on his right and Shell's head and paws peeped out of his coat pocket.

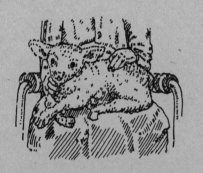

'I am going out in my chair this afternoon,' said Colin. 'If
the fresh air agrees with me I may go out every day. When I
go, none of the gardeners are to be anywhere near the Long
Walk by the garden walls. No one is to be there. I shall go out
about two o'clock and everyone must keep away until I send
word that they may go back to their work.'

'I shall get well! I shall get well! I shall get well!' he cried
out.

They drew the chair under the plum-tree, which was snow white with blossoms and musical with bees. It was like a king's canopy, a fairy king's.

'I don't want this afternoon to go,' he said; 'but I shall come back to-morrow, and the day after, and the day after, and the day after...I've seen the spring now and I'm going to see the summer. I'm going to see everything grow here. I'm going to grow here myself.'

...There was Ben Weatherstaff's indignant face glaring at them over the wall from the top of a ladder!

'If I wasn't a bachelder, an' tha' was a wench o' mine,' he cried, 'I'd give thee a hidin'!'

'It was the robin who showed me the way,' she protested
obstinately. 'He didn't know he was doing it, but he did. And I
can't tell you from here, while you're shaking your fist at me.'

...Colin was standing upright—upright—as straight as an arrow and looking strangely tall—his head thrown back and his strange eyes flashing lightning.

'Look at me!' he flung up at Ben Weatherstaff. 'Just look at me—you! Just look at me!'

'Eh!' he burst forth, 'th' lies folk tells! Tha'rt as thin as a lath an' as white as a wraith, but there's not a knob on thee. Tha'lt make a mon yet. God bless thee!'

'I'm your master,' he said, 'when my father is away. And you are to obey me. This is my garden. Don't dare to say a word about it! You get down from that ladder and go out to the Long Walk and Miss Mary will meet you and bring you here. I want to talk to you. We did not want you, but now you will have to be in the secret. Be quick!'

'...My orders are that no one is to know that we come here. Dickon and my cousin have worked and made it come alive. I shall send for you sometimes to help—but you must come when no one can see you.'

'Tha' said as tha'd have me walkin' about here same as other folk—an' tha' said tha'd have me diggin'. I thowt tha' was just leein' to please me. This is only th' first day an' I've walked—an' here I am diggin'.'

'...Tha'rt a Yorkshire lad for sure. An' tha'rt diggin', too. How'd tha' like to plant a bit o' somethin'? I can get thee a rose in a pot...'

'Here, lad,' he said, handing the plant to Colin. 'Set it in the earth thysel' same as th' king does when he goes to a new place.'

'...And the sun is only slipping over the edge. Help me up, Dickon. I want to be standing when it goes. That's part of the Magic.'

Dr. Craven had been waiting some time at the house when they returned to it.

'You should not have stayed so long,' he said. 'You must not over exert yourself.'

The seeds Dickon and Mary had planted grew as if fairies had tended them.

Colin saw it all, watching each change as it took place. Every morning he was brought out and every hour of each day, when it didn't rain he spent in the garden.

'Good morning, Ben Weatherstaff,' he said. 'I want you and Dickon and Miss Mary to stand in a row and listen to me because I am going to tell you something very important.

'I am going to try a scientific experiment,' explained the rajah. 'When I grow up I am going to make great scientific discoveries and I am going to begin now with this experiment.

'...The Magic in this garden has made me stand up and know I am going to live to be a man. I am going to make the scientific experiment of trying to get some and put it in myself and make it push and draw me and make me strong...I am going to say, "Magic is in me! Magic is making me well..!" And you must all do it, too. That is my experiment. Will you help, Ben Weatherstaff?'

...Fired by recollections of fakirs and devotees in illustrations Colin suggested that they should all sit cross-legged under the tree, which made a canopy.

'It will be like sitting in a sort of temple,' said Colin.

'...Shall we sway backward and forward, Mary, as if we were dervishes?'

...It really did look like a procession. Colin was at its head with Dickon on one side and Mary on the other. Ben Weatherstaff walked behind, and the "creatures" trailed after them...

From that time the exercises were part of the day's duties as much as the Magic was. It became possible for both Colin and Mary to do more of them each time they tried...

That afternoon Mary noticed that something new had happened in Colin's room. She had noticed it the day before, but had said nothing because she thought the change may have been made by chance. She said nothing to-day, but she sat and looked fixedly at the picture over the mantel. She could look at it because the curtain had been drawn aside.

Dear Sir,—

I am Susan Sowerby that made bold to speak to you once on the moor. It was about Miss Mary I spoke. I will make bold to speak again. Please, sir, I would come home if I was you. I think you would be glad to come and—if you will excuse me, sir—I think your lady would ask you to come if she was here,

Your obedient servant,

Susan Sowerby.

He had not meant to be a bad father, but he had not felt like a father at all. He had supplied doctors and nurses and luxuries, but he had shrunk from the mere thought of the boy and had buried himself in his own misery.

'How is Master Colin, Medlock?' he inquired.

'Well, sir,' Mrs. Medlock answered, 'he's—he's different, in a manner of speaking.'

'Worse?' he suggested.

Mrs. Medlock really was flushed.

'Well, you see, sir,' she tried to explain, 'neither Dr. Craven, nor the nurse, nor me can exactly make him out.'

'Father,' he said, 'I'm Colin. You can't believe it. I scarcely can myself. I'm Colin.'

Like Mrs. Medlock, he did not understand what his father meant when he said hurriedly:

'In the garden! In the garden!'

'Yes,' hurried on Colin. 'It was the garden that did it—and Mary and Dickon and the creatures—and the Magic. No one knows. We kept it to tell you when you came. I'm well; I can beat Mary in a race. I'm going to be an athlete.'

'Take me into the garden, my boy,' he said at last. 'And tell me all about it.'

And so they led him in.

The place was a wilderness of autumn gold and purple and violet blue and flaming scarlet, and on every side were sheaves of late lilies standing together—lilies which were white or white and ruby. He remembered well when the first of them had been planted that just at this season of the year their late glories should reveal themselves.

'Now,' he said at the end of the story, 'it need not be a secret any more. I dare say it will frighten them nearly into fits when they see me—but I am never going to get into the chair again. I shall walk back with you, Father—to the house.'

Published in the USA in 1995 by Sterling Publishing Company, Inc.,
387 Park Avenue South, New York, NY 10016
and by Museum Quilts Publications, Inc.
Published in the UK by Museum Quilts (UK) Inc.,
254-258 Goswell Road, London EC1V 7EB
Distributed in Canada by Sterling Publishing
c/o Canadian Manda Group, One Atlantic Avenue, Suite 105
Toronto, Ontario, Canada M6K 3E7
Distributed in Australia by
Capricorn Link (Australia) Pty Ltd.,
P.O. Box 6651, Baulkham Hills, Business Centre,
NSW 2153, Australia

ISBN: 0-8069-3974-5

Printed and bound in Korea